"Jay Earley knows what makes a care[t] *Caretaking*, he has named what goes [o] the mechanisms and triggers that lea[d] mode and the motivations behind th[e] is that when I come from unhealthy [c] the person I'm trying to help and can [?] pattern, their addiction. That alone is ..o...........p.......o.. admission.

CW00920463

"The book helped me to see that I may be inviting unhealthy people into my life because of this pattern, and the consequences for me are resentment and fatigue. All this was written in a way that was sensitive to my experience as the reader. The book outlines solutions systematically and provides easy, step-by-step instructions to follow to create changes in this pattern. Bottom line—it is a very thorough, effective piece of work."

— John Madatian, Gestalt practitioner

"*Beyond Caretaking* helped clarify the dual nature of caring and caretaking. The workbook further clarified which activity I am prone to. This clarification made it easier to choose a healthier pattern of behavior without being tripped up by guilt. Earley's arguments for caring vs. self-care are reasonable, sensible, and resonate internally. He presents his perspective on the link between present actions and childhood wounds in a very gentle manner that educates without filling the reader with regret and desire for avoidance. The book is simple, whetted my appetite to know more about the Pattern System, and kept me engaged enough to finish it in one sitting."

— Sydney Zink, PhD

"I found *Beyond Caretaking* well worth spending time with. I learned a lot about myself, particularly why I am a caretaker in the first place. It helps you to become aware of what triggers you to jump in and take care of everything. The process of changing and developing self-care is broken down into easy steps that I found very useful."

— Ines Hasenfuss

Beyond Caretaking

Balancing Giving with Self-Care

Jay Earley, PhD

 PATTERN SYSTEM BOOKS

Larkspur, CA

Beyond Caretaking: Balancing Giving with Self-Care

Copyright © 2012 by Jay Earley.
All right reserved.

Without limiting the rights under copyright reserved above,
no part of this publication may be reproduced, stored in or
introduced into a retrieval system, or transmitted, in any form or
by any means (electronic, mechanical, photocopying, recording,
or otherwise), without the prior written permission of both the
copyright owner and the above publisher of this book.

▦ PATTERN SYSTEM BOOKS

140 Marina Vista Ave.
Larkspur, CA 94939
415-924-5256
www.patternsystembooks.com

Paperback ISBN-13: 978-0-9855937-5-9
LCCN: 2012949582

Printed in the United States of America

Introduction to the Pattern System Series

This is a series of books that are based on the *Pattern System*SM—a comprehensive mapping of the human psyche. You can use the Pattern System to obtain a complete map of your psyche. You will be able to see your strengths and your defenses, your places of pain and how you compensate for them. You'll come to understand the structure of your inner conflicts and see where you are ready to grow. The Pattern System makes clear what you need to explore next in order to resolve the issues that are most important to you.

You'll learn where there is underlying pain, shame, or fear that must be healed. You'll also learn which healthy psychological capacities you can develop (or are already developing) to become happier and more productive.

In the Pattern System, *patterns* represent dysfunctional behaviors that cause problems for us or other people. *Healthy capacities* are the ways we feel and act that make our lives productive, connected, and happy. The Pattern System organizes the patterns and capacities according to various psychological *dimensions*, such as intimacy, power, and self-esteem.

Once you learn the basics of the Pattern System, if you choose to explore more deeply, you'll learn other concepts. At a deeper level are *motivations*, which are the types of intentions underlying your behavior and which are often unconscious. They are derived from the hurtful ways you were treated in childhood, which are represented by *wounds*.

Each book covers one pattern and the corresponding healthy capacity that is needed to break free of it. In the process of learning about each pattern, you can delve into its motivations and the wounds behind them. This will help you to transform your way of living from the pattern to the capacity.

See http://thepatternsystem.wikispaces.com for an outline and fuller description of the Pattern System.

Acknowledgments

I am grateful for helpful suggestions from Ines Hassen-fuss, Sefali Bhutwala, Sydney Zink, and Bonnie Weiss.

I appreciate the sharp eyes and clear mind of Kira Freed, who provided quality editing as well as interior design for the paperback version. As always, I love the clear aesthetic that Jeannene Langford brings to cover design.

Rachel Whalley created the workbook and provided great ideas for the icons in the Interpersonal Patterns graphic. Charlie Alolkoy and Kira Freed collaborated on creating this graphic. Kathy Wilber has done an excellent job on the programming behind the workbook.

Contents

Introduction

Do you find yourself always concerned about other people's needs? Do you feel that your needs don't really count? Do you feel as though you have to take care of other people's feelings, but no one seems to care about yours? Are you surrounded by people who need you? Is your self-worth dependent on being needed?

If you answered yes to some of these questions, you are one of the many people struggling with the Caretaking Pattern. Of course, it's a good thing to be caring and helpful to people and make them feel good, but maybe you go overboard in this direction.

Do you go out of your way to make sure that you don't cause anyone discomfort? Do you find yourself trying to help someone with an addiction, but you just enable them to continue? Do you believe that you know better than other people how they should run their lives?

Your urge to take care of people may come more from a need for self-esteem or a fear of being rejected or judged than from simple, heartfelt caring. You may be completely ignoring your own needs in favor of everyone else's. You may not really be helping the people you care about. You might even be infantilizing someone by not believing that they can handle their own life.

If you are tired of this pattern and would like to make a change, this book is for you. It will help you understand the fears and needs that are behind your Caretaking and where they come from in your past. It will help you learn how to become more attentive to your own needs and trust other people to take care of themselves. You can make this change without giving up your genuine caring for people.

This book will help you to know what you need and to take initiative to get it, while still being attentive to other people's needs. You will have an equal say in what happens, and people will take you seriously.

This doesn't mean that you will stop caring about other people and wanting the best for them. However, you won't be doing this from a place of fear or need. When you do care for people and help them to feel good, it will come purely from a loving place in you. You will care for yourself and your needs as well, and you'll also be respecting other people's ability to take care of themselves.

You will develop the ability to look out for yourself while still being a kind and loving person.

The Pattern System and
Internal Family Systems Therapy

This book is primarily based on the Pattern System (see Introduction to the Pattern System Series). Internal Family Systems Therapy (IFS) is an extremely powerful and user-friendly form of psychotherapy that I use and teach. IFS and the Pattern System complement each other. The Pattern System provides a theory of the psychological content of the human psyche, while IFS provides a powerful method for the healing and transformation of psychological problems.

I have chosen to write this book in such a way that you don't need to understand anything about IFS or parts. For those of you who already know IFS, the concepts in this book are completely compatible with it and can enhance your IFS work on yourself. In Chapter 9, I explain how IFS can be helpful in enhancing the work described in this book.

How to Use This Book

You can use this book to explore either your own Caretaking Pattern or that of another person. The book is written in terms of the reader's pattern, but you can easily apply what you learn to other people. Chapter 2 is for those of you who are reading this specifically to learn about another person.

Visit http://www.personal-growth-programs.com/ beyond-caretaking to register yourself as an owner of this book. As I write subsequent books in this series, I keep noticing improvements I want to make in previous books. If you register as an owner of this book, every time I improve the book, I will email you the latest ebook version.[1] You will also be notified about each new book in the series as it comes out.

Even though this book is a workbook, there is also a workbook on the web at http://www.personalgrowthapplica tion.com/Pattern/CaretakingWorkbook/Caretaking_ Workbook.aspx that goes with this book. There are many places in the book where you can check off items or fill in blanks. You have a choice of doing this directly in this book or using the web workbook instead. All the information

---

1. I will send you a Kindle version, which you can read on your computer, tablet, or smartphone using free software that you can download from Amazon.

in the web workbook will be held under your name and password with complete confidentiality and security. At any point, you will be able to return to the web workbook to look at your answers, change them, or print them out. You will be able to use either workbook to engage in the life practice in Chapter 7.

This book is aimed at helping you change. Therefore, it is crucial that you fill out this workbook or the web workbook and do the practice to change your Caretaking Pattern.

We are forming a Caretaking Online Community of people who are reading this book and would like to support each other in letting go of excessive Caretaking. You can find the Online Community at http://www.personal-growth-programs.com/connect. We will help you find a buddy to talk with as you are reading the book, and especially to help you engage in the life practice in Chapter 7 and to support you in taking care of yourself. You can also participate in discussions and phone meetings where you share your struggles and triumphs with others who are dealing with the same issues around Caretaking. The meetings and discussions will be facilitated by myself or a colleague, and we will be available to answer questions of yours that come up.

This support could make all the difference in your success at using this book to work through Caretaking and develop more Self-Care. It is part of a larger community of people who are working on personal growth and healing through our books, websites, and programs.

Many different patterns are mentioned at various points in this book. Most of these are just for you to explore in more detail if you choose to. If you just want to move ahead to get help with your Caretaking Pattern, feel free to ignore these patterns. It isn't important that you remember or understand them. Just keep reading to get the help you want.

I congratulate you on your willingness to embark on this exciting inner journey. You will soon discover how the Caretaking Pattern operates, the unconscious motives behind it, and where they likely came from in your childhood. You will discover how to transform this pattern so you can balance your care for others and yourself. You will also explore the various aspects of the Self-Care Capacity and how to cultivate them.

6   *Beyond Caretaking*

CHAPTER 1

Your Caretaking Pattern

If you have the Caretaking Pattern, you are caring and compassionate toward others, but often at the expense of your own needs or desires. If you have this pattern strongly, you will find yourself constantly taking care of others financially, logistically, and emotionally. At some level, though, your caring comes with some strings attached. You have a deep desire to be appreciated for all that you give to others, rather than giving without concern about what you get back. You may hope that people will like you or not leave you in return for your efforts.

You may take pride in being a "mind reader." With a strong Caretaking Pattern, you get a lift from providing assistance that you believe people need, even before they ask for it. You may frequently give too much help, and often at the expense of taking care of yourself. You may regularly be the last person to leave a party, even when you're exhausted, because you're always helping the host tidy up. You might even get so emotionally involved with someone's problem that you are more distressed about the problem than they are.

You may believe that all of your giving to others is building up a pool of help and favors that you can call upon someday. Or you may believe that by reading the minds of your loved ones, you will be able to expect them to do the same for you—that they will know and deliver the support you want without you ever having to ask.

Some level of the desire to help others is natural and healthy. We are, after all, social beings who need interpersonal support to get along in the world. But if you find yourself regularly sacrificing your own comfort for the sake of helping someone else—for instance, if you give up a therapeutic massage appointment because your sister "just has to have your opinion" on a new couch she's buying—you very likely have the Caretaking Pattern.

In fact, your Caretaking part may assume that other people aren't as capable of taking care of themselves as you are. You might believe that you "know better" when it comes to what would be good for someone else. Unless this person is a small child, though, it is unlikely that your perception of someone else's needs is more valid than their own.

For a variety of reasons, you may not have received feedback from others that your Caretaking is a problem. If you have the Caretaking Pattern, you probably attract people who may, on some level, like being taken care of or who become dependent on you. If you have a Caretaking Pattern, you may have people in your life whom you believe would suffer if you were to stop caretaking them, and you may have a sense of enjoying "being needed."

The key to knowing if you have the Caretaking Pattern is to look at how often you are meeting your own needs. If you are always putting yourself last, or if you are tired and feel as though you are responsible for making sure other people are okay emotionally, logistically, or financially, you have the Caretaking Pattern.

The Caretaking Pattern often presents a struggle for parents. When your children are young, it is appropriate for you to be a Caretaker for them because they can't do many things for themselves, and you are responsible for them. As they grow and mature, you have the tricky task of gradually letting go of your caretaking as they become more capable of taking care of themselves. And today when many adult children still live at home, this transition has added complications.

This is especially difficult for mothers. How can you continue to love your children and want the best for them while allowing them to gradually take responsibility for themselves to the extent that they can, including making potentially costly mistakes? Many mothers have a hard time making this shift as soon as it is needed, so they end up with a Caretaking Pattern with their teenage or adult children.

False Belief of the Caretaking Pattern: I am responsible for other people's feelings. I must do what I can to make them happy and keep them from feeling pain or discomfort.

A Story of a Caretaking Pattern

Carolyn was well liked by her friends. If anyone ever needed a hand, she was there to help. She brought amazing food to every potluck, she staffed back-to-back shifts at charity raffle tables, and she was always available with a tissue and a hug whenever any of her friends was having a hard time.

CAROLYN: "I know that everyone likes having me around. And I like being needed. But yeah, sometimes I do get kinda worn out. Sometimes I wish I had more time to take care of myself … but there's always somebody's play to go to or someone who just broke up with her boyfriend. There's not really a day that goes by when there isn't something going on that I need to be there for."

Carolyn doesn't just offer help and support to her friends—she also takes care of people in her family. Lately, she has been struggling with her younger sister and has begun to wonder if her sister takes advantage of her.

CAROLYN: "I care about Melissa—I do. But sometimes I get frustrated with how helpless she seems to be. I mean,

I understand if she needs a little money now and then. I've done well for myself, and I can afford to help her out a bit. If I have to postpone my vacation, it's not that big of a deal. But no matter how many times I help her by pointing her in the direction of a good job, picking out what she should wear, and helping her figure out what to say in an interview, she just never seems to get it together. She might have a good job for a couple of months, but it never pans out, and then she's calling me for help all over again."

One of Carolyn's friends pointed out to her that she might be "enabling" her sister, which means, in this case, encouraging her to be dependent and not grow up. Carolyn protested at first and then had a realization.

CAROLYN: "I worry about what would happen to Melissa without my help. She's not so good at taking care of herself. Yeah, she's 32 now, but she's always been my baby sister, and I've always looked out for her. The more I think about it though, honestly, while she drives me crazy, I kinda don't know how I'd feel if she stopped needing me. That's always been our relationship. I don't know how I'd fit into her life if things were different. But maybe how I treat her is part of the problem. Maybe she isn't going to learn how to live like an adult if I'm always taking care of her. And maybe I wouldn't be so frustrated with her if I weren't so worried about how to help her all the time."

Carolyn's story will be continued later in the book.

Caretaking Behaviors and Feelings

The following are common behaviors and feelings that come from the Caretaking Pattern. Which of these apply to you?

❏ I care for others more than myself.

❏ I care for others at my own expense.

❏ I am invested in being a helper.

❏ I can't say no to requests for help.

❏ I am drawn to people who need help.

❏ I try to be the savior of troubled people.

❏ I try to keep peace between others and be a go-between.

❏ I try to placate people so they don't fight with each other.

❏ I feel guilty for not doing enough to help others.

❏ I go overboard to not hurt others or make them feel bad.

❏ I am codependent.

❏ I get emotionally involved in other people's problems.

❏ I try to make things easy on others, even when this isn't best for them.

❏ I believe that I know what is best for someone better than they do.

❏ I may try to impose my help on other people.

❏ I am sometimes more upset about someone's problem than they are.

❏ If I spend much time with a friend or lover, I believe I owe it to them to continue the relationship.

❏ I take on other people's pain in an attempt to heal them.

❐ Other behavior _____

_____

❐ Other feelings _____

_____

If you prefer to use a workbook on the web rather than filling out your answers in this book or on paper, visit http://www.personalgrowthapplication.com/Pattern/CaretakingWorkbook/Caretaking_Workbook_Behaviors_and_Thoughts.aspx.

You don't have to engage in all these behaviors to have the Caretaking Pattern. And for the ones you do have, you don't have to be doing them all the time.

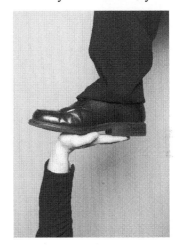

Your Caretaking Pattern might be operating all the time, or it might be triggered only under certain circumstances, such as when a family member has a compelling need for money or a friend is in a difficult relationship. Think about the circumstances that tend to trigger your Caretaking.

Caretaking Thoughts

If you listen carefully to your thoughts, you may become aware of ones that are related to Caretaking. Here are some examples. Which ones resonate with you, and in which situations do they tend to come up?

❏ Be friendly and nice to everyone.

❏ Try to make that person happy.

❏ You are responsible for that person's well-being.

❏ You are responsible for whatever goes on in this group.

❏ You are responsible for solving the world's problems.

❏ You should feel guilty for not doing more for people.

❏ You should feel bad for making that person feel uncomfortable.

❏ If you can't say anything nice, don't say anything at all.

❏ You must make that person feel better.

❏ It's your job to make people happy.

❏ How can you sit by and let those people suffer? You must do something.

❏ Other behavior _____

_____

❏ Other feelings _____

_____

Situations That Trigger Caretaking

What are typical situations that trigger your Caretaking Pattern—in other words, when do you lose your center of gravity and go into full-on giving mode? For example, when a boyfriend or girlfriend is in emotional pain, when family members are having a conflict, with a friend who needs a lot of support, when an adult child is unemployed? List the situations in which you go into Caretaking mode. Be very specific—for example, when your date feels neglected or hurt, when a parent feels overwhelmed, or when a coworker asks for your advice. You will process them later in the book.

_____

_____

_____

_____

Types of Caretaking Patterns

There are a number of different kinds of Caretaking Patterns. Check off the ones that are closest to yours.

☐ Conflict-Avoiding

You are frightened of conflict and do your best to avoid it because you don't want to hurt anyone or cause them discomfort. If someone confronts you or brings up a conflictual issue, you usually just give in to them in order to avoid any difficulties. You immediately take the blame without even considering whether or not you are to blame—anything to end the argument.

If there is something that is bothering you about a friend's behavior, you avoid bringing it up with them, no matter how uncomfortable it makes you feel. You may not even let yourself know that it bothers you so you don't feel any conflict about not dealing with it.[2]

---

2. In this case, you have the Conflict-Avoiding Pattern (http://www.personal-growth-programs.com/conflict-avoiding-pattern) as well as the Caretaking Pattern. Follow this link (and those throughout the rest of the book) to see if the book for this pattern is now available.

❐ Codependent

You are close to someone with an addiction, and you hate to see them in pain, so you try to help them out, but the way you do this just enables their addiction. For example, a relative is addicted to gambling or shopping and constantly runs out of money and comes to you for "loans." You keep giving them money, even though they never repay you, and this just feeds their addiction.

❐ Controlling

You believe that you know what is best for other people better than they do, and you try to get them to do it. You feel that your wisdom is crucial to their ability to live their lives, and you don't trust them to make the right decisions. You may become controlling and judgmental in order to try to coerce people into taking your advice. You might even be invested in having people depend on your caretaking because this gives you power over them. This type of caretaking may generate anger and defiance in the people you are trying to help.[3]

Here is an example. Darien felt that he knew what career was best for his son, Bill. He should become a lawyer or a doctor, or something of equal status and earning power. Darien felt that this was very important to Bill's having a happy life. He made this very clear to Bill and wasn't very interested in what Bill's talents were or what Bill really wanted to devote his life to. It wasn't simply that Darien was controlling. He really did care about Bill and want the best for him. It's just that he didn't trust Bill to know what that was.

When Bill decided that he wanted to be a musician, Darien was appalled, and they had many fights about it. Bill went ahead with his music career anyway, and after a number of years, he realized that he couldn't really make a living at it. Darien was right there with "I told you so."

Bill then decided that he wanted to be an acupuncturist, and their fights started all over again. Again Bill went ahead and got trained in acupuncture, and this time he ended up making quite a good living for himself in that career and really enjoyed his work. Eventually Darien had to admit that he hadn't known what was best for Bill, and they were able to reconnect, but their relationship had to go through years of turmoil first because of Darien's controlling Caretaking Pattern.

---

3. In this case, you have the Controlling Pattern (http://www.personal-growth-programs.com/controlling-pattern) as well as the Caretaking Pattern.

☐ People Pleasing

You go out of your way to make other people happy, even when it means making yourself unhappy. Your needs and well-being don't count—only those of other people. You give other people the best seat, the best portion of food, and so on. You often make special arrangements to make someone happy.[4]

☐ Basic Caretaking

You do your best to take care of other people, especially if they are in pain or if something you might do could cause them pain or discomfort. You always want to be there to nurture and support them, no matter what it costs you.

Notice that some of these types are related to other patterns, which you might need to explore to work through your Caretaking. Click on the links on these patterns to see which of those books are available now.

Please don't feel that you have to remember all the different patterns and capacities that are introduced in this book. Just explore the ones that are relevant for you. The Pattern System will gradually make sense the more you use it. To see an overview of the whole system, read Appendix A or visit http://thepatternsystem.wikispaces.com.

---

4. In this case, you have the People-Pleasing Pattern (http://www.personal-growth-programs.com/people-pleasing-pattern) as well as the Caretaking Pattern.

As you read about these patterns that you might have (and others later in the book), please don't judge yourself because you may have some of them. We all have a variety of different patterns of relating that don't work for us. There is nothing deficient or wrong with you because you have some—in fact, just the opposite. You are reading this book because you are interested in learning about yourself and changing your patterns. You are to be congratulated for your commitment to self-awareness.

At this point, if you aren't sure whether you have the Caretaking Pattern or another pattern related to Care, read Chapter 8 and take the quiz on the Care Dimension.

CHAPTER 2

Other People's Patterns

How Your Caretaking Pattern
May Affect Other People

You may be attracted to people with a Dependent Pattern[5] or a Victim Pattern[6] because it fits so well with your desire to take care of people. However, in the long run, this probably won't work so well unless one or both of you work on changing your patterns. You may eventually get tired of always being the Caretaker, or your partner might get increasingly needy and clingy. You may resent the fact that you never get your needs attended to.

If you become an enabler to someone with an addiction, this isn't good for either of you. You may find yourself trying to control other

5. http://www.personal-growth-programs.com/dependent-pattern
6. http://www.personal-growth-programs.com/victim-pattern

people's lives or help them even when they don't want your help. This will most likely cause resentment. The other possibility is that you will encourage someone to become dependent on you because of your need to be the Caretaker, and this will stunt their growth.

You might also find yourself connecting with a person with an Entitled,[7] Controlling,[8] or Deceptive[9] Pattern because you might be too focused on taking care of them to be aware of how you are being controlled, used, or deceived, and this could even lead to being abused. This is especially likely to happen if your parents had one or more of these patterns.

You might perceive someone with the Self-Support Capacity as being distant because you want them to need you, and you see need as intimacy. When someone doesn't need you very much because of healthy Self-Support, you might misperceive this as an avoidance of intimacy.

If Someone Close to You Is a Caretaker

If you suspect that someone close to you has a Caretaking Pattern, you may be reading this book to try and understand their behavior and feelings. This can be very helpful in getting clear on where this person is coming from.

In addition, this book can help you understand yourself more deeply. It is possible that you are inadvertently contributing to this person's Caretaking by being needy and dependent. Consider whether or not this might be the case before trying to change this person.

---

7. http://www.personal-growth-programs.com/entitled-pattern
8. http://www.personal-growth-programs.com/controlling-pattern
9. http://www.personal-growth-programs.com/deceptive-pattern

How to Relate to a Caretaker

If you are close to someone who is a Caretaker, there are some things you can do to minimize this tendency in them. Try to avoid triggering this person's fears that lead to Caretaking. Read Chapter 3 and Chapter 4 to get a sense of which underlying fears this person might have that lead them to be a Caretaker. Talk with them to get a better sense of what they might be afraid of. This will help you to be aware of times when you unintentionally trigger this person's fears.

For example, if this person is afraid of being rejected if they don't take care of you, be on the lookout for anything you might say that contains any hint of rejection. Even if this person is overly sensitive to abandonment, you can maximize the chances of him or her feeling safe with you by watching what you say.

If this person hints that you are being rejecting, stop for a moment to consider what they are saying and see if this is true. See if you can become aware of such behavior in the future so you stop acting it out. You can even make a point of being explicitly accepting and reassuring to this person.

In the end, if this person continues to be overly caretaking toward you, simply refuse to allow him or her to take care of you in ways that you don't want.

CHAPTER 3

The Underlying Motivation
for Caretaking

Outline of the Change Process

The next five chapters constitute the heart of the change process for Caretaking. Here is an outline:

- Chapters 3 & 4: Understand underlying motivations (mainly fears) for Caretaking and their origins in childhood.

- Chapter 5: Work through these fears so your Caretaking begins to let go.

- Chapter 6: Explore the Self-Care Capacity that you will develop to replace Caretaking.

- Chapter 7: Engage in a life practice to make this happen.

Motivations for Caretaking

In order to change your Caretaking Pattern, it is very helpful to understand the underlying motivation behind it and its origins in your childhood.

There are many reasons that a pattern like this might develop. Some are outlined here. You may take care of others because you are afraid of being emotionally harmed or rejected if you don't. You might also be trying to get acceptance, approval, caring, or love by being a Caretaker. Or you might be afraid of something bad happening to people if you stop being their primary support.

Some of your fears might be conscious, but others can be deeply buried. You might even know that there is no real danger if you stop being a Caretaker, but an unconscious part of you is still afraid of it.

This chapter introduces another concept from the Pattern System. *Motivations* are the underlying reasons behind your patterns—what drives them. Your motivations might involve fears, rebellion, or other intentions.

How to Approach This Information

There is potentially painful material to explore in this chapter and the next one. Take it slowly and make sure that you are OK emotionally. Take a break any time you feel the need. Call a friend to talk about the feelings that are coming up, if that would help you feel supported through this process.

As you read through these motivations and think about the ones that pertain to you, please don't judge yourself. It is common for our Inner Critics to use this information to make us feel bad about ourselves. They tell us that we are really screwed up, that we'll never have love. Don't believe these self-attacks.

Keep in mind that everyone has a host of fears, needs, and other underlying motivations for their behavior. And everyone has had a variety of childhood wounds. We don't all have the same wounds and fears, but we all have plenty of them. It is perfectly normal to have a variety of these issues.

You aren't bad or pathological or inadequate because of the ones you have. If your Inner Critic is beating you up about your fears, let it know that judgment isn't helpful. When you can take in new information from an open place, it helps you to see yourself more clearly.

Adopt an attitude of looking at yourself objectively and compassionately as you explore your motivations and wounds. This approach is enormously helpful in learning about yourself. You had to develop these patterns of defense because of the ways you were wounded when you were very young and vulnerable. They aren't your fault. Appreciate yourself for being interested in delving into this material so you can stop being a Caretaker.

Motivations

Let's look at the different motivations for being a Caretaker to see which ones resonate with you. Look over the following to see which ones apply to you. If you aren't sure, read the next chapter for more details about each of these motivations and where they come from in childhood.

Fear of Harm

❐ I am afraid of being yelled at or hit if I don't take care of people.

❐ I am afraid of being criticized if I don't take care of people.

❐ I am afraid of being shamed if I don't take care of people.

❐ I am afraid of being betrayed if I don't take care of people.

Fear of Rejection

❐ I am afraid of being rejected if I don't take care of people.

❐ I am afraid of not being cared for or being abandoned if I don't take care of people.

❐ I am afraid of being dismissed, discounted, or not valued if I don't take care of people.

Attempt to Get Connection

❐ I am trying to get acceptance and interest by taking care of people so I don't feel unlikable.

❐ I am trying to get approval and admiration by taking care of people so I feel good about myself and don't feel deficient.

❐ I am trying to get love by taking care of people so I don't feel unlovable.

❐ I am trying to get caring by taking care of people so I don't feel deprived and abandoned.

Other Fears

❐ I am afraid that I will feel guilty if I don't take care of people.

❐ I am afraid that if I don't take care of people, they will collapse because they can't take care of themselves.

❐ I am afraid of feeling my pain if I don't take away other people's pain.

Belief in Caretaking

❐ I believe it's right to take care of people.

In Service of the Controlling Pattern

❐ If I take care of people, it gives me the power in the situation.

Being the Opposite of a Parent

❐ My mother (or father) was so selfish and uncaring that it made my life difficult or was embarrassing to me, so I swore that I would never be like that. I went to the opposite extreme and tried to take care of everyone.

The next chapter goes into more detail about each of these motivations and their origins in your childhood situation.

CHAPTER 4

Details About Motivations
and Childhood Origins

For each type of motivation from the previous chapter, there is a section in this chapter with more detail about that motivation and the childhood situation it comes from.

There are a number of different ways to use this chapter.

1. If you already have a pretty good idea about your motivations, you can skip this chapter and perhaps come back to it later to explore where they come from in your childhood.

2. You can go directly to those motivations you checked off in the previous chapter and only explore them.

3. You can read through the entire chapter to get a fuller understanding of your motivations and where they come from. However, if all the detail doesn't feel helpful right now, feel free to skip to the next chapter and come back to this one at a later time.

This chapter introduces two more concepts from the Pattern System. *Wounds* and *origins* are the ways you were treated when you were a child that led to your dysfunctional patterns of behavior as an adult. *Wounds* refer to the pain underlying your motivations, while *origins* refer to the ways your behavior was shaped in childhood.

How to Approach This Material

Caution: There is a lot of detailed and potentially painful material to explore in this chapter. Feel free to stop at any point when you feel you have processed enough for the moment or for today. Take it slowly and make sure that you are OK emotionally. Take a break any time you feel the need. It often helps to process things gradually. When you sit for a while with something difficult, you can digest it more easily, like a big meal. Call a friend or your buddy from the Caretaking Online Community to talk about the feelings that are coming up, if that would help you feel supported through this process.

Many motivations and wounds are named in this chapter. It isn't important that you remember or understand them all—only the ones that are relevant to your Caretaking Pattern. Feel free to ignore the others and just focus on understanding where your Caretaking comes from.

If you have more than one of these motivations and

wounds, don't try to process them all at once. Monitor yourself so you can process what you are learning and so you don't get overwhelmed emotionally. Just look at some of them, and come back to the others later.

If two or three of these motivations or wounds seem similar to you, don't worry about teasing them out—just check off all of them. For example, if shame and dismissal seem similar to you, it is probably because you were both shamed and dismissed. Just check off both of them, and then, in Chapter 7, process them together.

Now let's begin with the first motivation.

Fear of Harm

You might be afraid of being harmed in some way (for example, criticized, shamed, or yelled at) if you stop Caretaking and care more for yourself. Of course, it is possible that you have been harmed for focusing on your own needs, but most likely this fear comes at least partly from your underlying issues.

There are five things you might be afraid of, and each is related to a wound. Look them over to see which one fits your Caretaking Pattern. You might have more than one.

☐ Fear of Being Yelled At or Hit

You might be afraid of being yelled at or hit if you don't take care of others.

This is related to the *Attack Wound*. When you were little, your parents (or others) may have yelled at you because you took care of your needs before theirs. They may even have abused you physically for not taking care of them in some way. Now you might be frightened of being treated that way again.

❐ Fear of Being Criticized

You might be afraid of being criticized if you don't take care of others.

This is related to the *Deficiency Wound.* When you were a child, you may have been criticized and made to feel inadequate for not trying to take care of others. This criticism may have come from your parents, siblings, or someone else you were close to. You might be afraid of this happening again in your adult life.

❐ Fear of Being Shamed

You might be afraid of being shamed if you don't take care of others.

This is related to the *Shame Wound.* When you were little, you may have been ridiculed, shamed, or embarrassed by parents or others you were close to if you placed your own needs above those of other people. You might be afraid of this being repeated in your adult life.

❐ Fear of Being Betrayed

You might be afraid of being betrayed if you don't take care of others.

This is related to the *Betrayal Wound.* When you were young, you may have trusted your parents, and one of them turned on you when you didn't tune in to their needs perfectly. Or perhaps a parent who really loved you occasionally became very nasty and hurtful when you shifted your focus away from their needs, and because you were open to him or her, it hurt that much more. This memory may make you wary of letting your attention stray from other people's needs.

Soothing Your Pain

As you read through these descriptions of childhood experiences, painful emotions may come up. It is helpful to soothe yourself when this happens. The best way to do this is to treat each painful emotion as coming from a child part of you—an inner child who was wounded when you were young.

Take a moment to contact this child inside of you. You may see an image of this inner child or feel him or her in your body, or just have a sense of the child. Open your heart to this little being. Be the compassionate, nurturing parent that this wounded inner child needs right now. Listen to his or her pain with caring. Imagine holding this child in your arms. Let the child know that you are there for him or her. Give this inner child the love he or she needs. And give the child whatever else he or she may need.

- Acceptance: "I accept you just the way you are."

- Validation: "You are a good person."

- Encouragement: "You can do it."

- Support: "I am standing behind you 100%."

- Appreciation: "You are very precious to me."

This will keep you from being overwhelmed by the pain that is coming up, and it may even help to heal that wound in you.

To listen to a guided meditation for nurturing this wounded inner child, visit http://www.personalgrowth application.com/Pattern/CaretakingWorkbook/Care taking_Workbook_Inner_Child_Meditation.aspx.

Fear of Rejection

You might be afraid of being rejected in some way if you don't take care of others or if you focus on your own needs. Of course, it is possible that you have been rejected for taking care of yourself, but most likely this fear comes at least partly from your underlying issues.

There are three major types of rejection in the Pattern System, and each is related to a wound. Look them over to see which one fits your Caretaking Pattern. You might have more than one.

❐ Fear of Being Rejected

You may be afraid of being rejected in some way if you don't take care of others.

This is related to the *Unlovable Wound.* When you were a child, your parents, siblings, or friends may have rejected you when you didn't focus on their needs, and you ended up feeling unlovable. Now you might fear that happening again.

❐ Fear of Not Being Cared For or Being Abandoned

You might be afraid of not being cared for or being abandoned if you don't take care of others.

This is related to the *Deprivation Wound.* You may not have gotten the love and care that you needed when you were young, and your parents said or implied that this was because you were inconsiderate. Or you may have been abandoned by your parents at a time when you really needed them, and they gave you the impression that it was because you were too self-centered. They may even have blamed you for not meeting  some need of theirs. Now you might be trying to get this love and caring by continually trying hard to earn "points" with them.

❐ **Fear of Being Dismissed, Discounted, or Not Valued**

You may be afraid of being dismissed, discounted, or not valued if you don't take care of others.

This is related to the *Deficiency Wound,* which is described above.

Attempt to Get Connection

You may be trying to get acceptance, approval, love, or caring by Caretaking. There are four major ways this can happen in the Pattern System, and each is related to a wound. Look them over to see which one fits your Caretaking Pattern. You might have more than one.

❐ **Attempt to Get Acceptance and Interest**

You may be trying to get acceptance and interest by taking care of people who are important to you so you don't feel unlikable or unacceptable.

This is related to the *Unlovable Wound,* which is described above.

❐ Attempt to Get Approval and Admiration

You might be trying to get approval and admiration by Caretaking so you feel good about yourself and don't feel deficient.

This is related to the *Deficiency Wound,* which is described above.

❐ Attempt to Get Love

You might be trying to get love by Caretaking so you don't feel unlovable.

This is related to the *Unlovable Wound,* which is described above.

❐ Attempt to Get Caring

You might be trying to get caring by Caretaking so you don't feel deprived and abandoned.

This is related to the *Deprivation Wound,* which is described above.

Other Fears

❐ Fear of Guilt

You might be afraid of feeling guilty if you don't take care of people.

This is related to the *Guilt Wound.* When you were a child, your parents may have made you feel guilty when you didn't take care of them or your brothers and sisters. Now you might fear that happening again if you don't take care of people.

❒ **Fear of People Collapsing**

You might be afraid that if you don't take care of people, they will collapse because they can't take care of themselves.

This is related to the *Deprivation Wound.* When you were a child, your parents may have collapsed many times despite your best efforts to take care of them. And when they collapsed, you had no one to take care of you, so you were abandoned and in need. You may have tried to take care of them in the hopes that they would then be able to take care of you. Now you might fear that happening again if you don't take care of people.

❒ **Fear of Feeling Your Pain**

You may be afraid of feeling your pain if you don't take away other people's pain. The pain of other people can trigger your own through empathy, so you may want to keep other people from feeling their pain to avoid having to feel yours.

This can relate to many different wounds, depending on what kind of pain you are carrying.

Belief in Caretaking

You may believe that it is right to be a Caretaker in relation to other people. There are five possible origins that could contribute to this belief.

Modeling Origin. One of your parents may have been a Caretaker, so you grew up assuming that that is the way a person should be.

Teaching Origin. Your parents or your religion may have told you how important it was to take care of people, so you came to believe that that is the way a person should be.

Reward Origin. Your parents may have rewarded you with praise whenever you took care of them or other people, so you came to believe that that is the way a person should be.

Punishment Origin. Your parents may have punished you when you didn't take care of them or other people, so you felt that you had to be a Caretaker in order to be safe.

Shaping Origin. Your need to be Caretaking may have been shaped by your childhood, which involved a combination of modeling, teaching, punishment, and/or reward.

In Service of the Controlling Pattern
You may have a need to be in control of situations and to be the one in power, which comes from the Controlling Pattern.[10] You try to take care of people because they will give you power over them.

Being the Opposite of a Parent
Your mother (or father) may have been so selfish and uncaring that it made your life difficult or embarrassed you, so you swore that you would never be like that.

---

10. In this case, you have the Controlling Pattern (http://www.personal-growth-programs.com/controlling-pattern) as well as the Caretaking Pattern.

Next Step

Whew! All of this chapter may have been hard to read. Yet it was necessary in order to come to an understanding of what motivates your Caretaking and where this tendency comes from in your past. This will be helpful to changing this pattern.

You should now have a pretty good idea of your motivations for Caretaking. Take your time and get emotional support to process these insights. It can be a lot to take on.

You are now prepared to change your Caretaking behavior, which starts in the next chapter.

CHAPTER 5

Working Through Caretaking Fears and Motivations

Now that you know which of your underlying fears are pushing you to take care of people, let's work them through.

When you are with a particular person or in a certain situation, your Caretaking Pattern may become activated. This pattern developed in childhood because you were dealing with a harmful situation, for example, being judged or yelled at, or because your needs weren't met unless you were taking care of others. And unconsciously, you believe that this is going to happen again.

However, your current situation is very different from what happened back then. You are no longer vulnerable and dependent like a child. You are most likely autonomous and no longer subject to the power of your parents. You have many strengths and capacities now as an adult (and possibly because of previous work you have done on yourself) that you didn't have as a child.

For example, you may be more grounded and centered. You may be able to assert yourself, be perceptive about interpersonal situations, support yourself financially, and so on. You have already accomplished many things in your life and overcome various obstacles. You are an adult with much more ability to handle yourself. You probably have friends, maybe a spouse or lover, perhaps a community you belong to, a support group, professionals you can rely on. You have people you can turn to if necessary.

This means that you aren't in danger the way you were as a child, and your mature self is more available, which wasn't possible when you were young. Therefore, it isn't really necessary for you to caretake any longer because this is a reaction to the past hurts and dangers.

In this chapter, you can work through the fears that lead to Caretaking. You can do this for any particular person or situation that leads to Caretaking. Choose one specific situation and apply the rest of this chapter to it. Then when you are finished with that situation, if you want, you can come back to this chapter and choose a different situation to process. I will call this the *Life Situation* for the chapter.

Are Your Fears Realistic?

First we will consider whether or not your fears or perceptions are accurate. Are the things you are afraid will happen if you aren't Caretaking really likely to happen? For example, if you are afraid of being judged if you don't take care of someone, consider whether this person would really judge you. If you are afraid of not getting acceptance or approval from someone unless you take care of them, consider whether or not this person might appreciate you anyway.

These questions aren't always easy to answer without bias. Consider them when you aren't emotionally triggered. Keep in mind that even though there may be a part of you that believes you will be harmed or rejected, this may not actually be the case. You might want to discuss this question with friends who know your situation.

If Your Fear Isn't Realistic

If you decide that you won't be harmed or rejected if you aren't Caretaking, this indicates that it is really safe for you to try it. What do you know about the Life Situation that makes your fear unrealistic?

_____

_____

_____

_____

_____

Carolyn's story is an example of this. Remember from Chapter 1 that Carolyn was a great friend to all and liked being needed but felt worn out from "being there" for everyone else all the time.

In exploring her Caretaking Pattern, Carolyn realized that she was afraid of not being liked and accepted if she didn't take care of others. When she looked into the childhood origins of this, she remembered that her mother withheld her love if Carolyn didn't take care of her younger brother and sister. She became frosty and self-contained if Carolyn wasn't willing to instantly drop what she was doing to attend to her siblings' needs. On the other hand, when Carolyn was available to take care of them, her mother showered her with appreciation and love. Carolyn learned that doing things for others was the only way to get love.

As Carolyn thought about it, she realized that she was no longer a little girl who was dependent on her mother's love. She realized that many of her friends would appreciate her and want to be close to her whether or not she was focusing on their needs all the time. She wasn't sure about a couple of friends or her sister, but she decided to practice being less of a Caretaker and more self-nurturing, and to see what would happen.

She began spending less time anticipating and filling the needs of her friends and more time focusing on her own well-being. Many of her friends responded well and supported her newfound self-care, and her connection with them improved. Carolyn really enjoyed discovering that these friends loved her for who she was—not just for what she could do for them.

However, there were other friends, as well as her sister, who had negative reactions to this change in Carolyn. We will look at how she handled these reactions later in this chapter.

If Your Fear Is Realistic

Even though your current situation is probably not as harmful as the childhood situation that produced your underlying fears, there may be some degree of validity to your fears. If this is the case, you want to separate out those fears and perceptions that are accurate from those that are not.

If there is some validity to your fear, take a moment to get in touch with exactly what you are afraid will or won't happen if you aren't taking care of others. Are you afraid that someone will criticize your intelligence? Are you afraid that someone will lose interest in you? Are you afraid they will feel hurt? Write what you are afraid will happen here:

_____

_____

_____

_____

_____

It is important to understand that you developed your relationships when you were Caretaking people too much, so your friends have come to expect this from you. Therefore, it isn't surprising that some of them may have reactions when you change what they have become accustomed to. Have compassion for their feelings since they need to adjust to your change in behavior and may feel hurt at first. Explain to them clearly why you want to make this change and show them that you understand how this might be hard for them. This will go a long way toward helping them to accept your new way of relating.[11]

Creating a Plan for This Fear

Make a plan for how you will handle the situation so that either the problems related to your fear won't happen or you will protect yourself if they do. Here are some possibilities:

1. You will assert yourself in such a way as to keep yourself from being hurt. For example, if someone pulls away from you for not caring enough for them, your plan will be to explain that you have been overdoing it and are just bringing some balance into the relationship. You have the right to attend to your needs, too.

2. You will sit down and talk with a person about changing his or her behavior so you aren't emotionally harmed or rejected. Do this at a time when you aren't in the middle of a conflict with this person. Explain how you are being hurt and make a request for the

---

11. You may need to work on developing your Assertiveness Capacity (http://www.personal-growth-programs.com/people-pleasing-pattern) to succeed at this.

person to respond differently. Of course, you should volunteer to listen to their concerns as well.[12]

3. If necessary, you will set limits that will prevent emotional harm. For example, if someone gets overly angry at you, you will say that the anger is inappropriate and demand that he or she stop or you will leave the situation.[13]

Work out this plan and write it here:

Then put it into operation and keep a record of your results. You may need to work through one of your patterns or develop a certain capacity for your plan to achieve the success you are looking for. Be aware that it may take time for the plan to succeed. Chapter 7 contains a practice to stop Caretaking that involves using your plan to make this safe.

Keep in mind that your fears may be partially realistic and partially not. In that case, you will need to adopt a strategy that is a mix of these two sections.

---

12. You may need to work on developing your Challenge Capacity (http://www.personal-growth-programs.com/conflict-avoiding-pattern) and Good Communication Capacity (http://www.personal-growth-programs.com/blaming-pattern) to have a successful conversation.

13. You may need to work on developing your Limit-Setting Capacity (http://www.personal-growth-programs.com/limit-setting-capacity) for this plan to succeed.

Carolyn's Relationships with Tammy and Jane

As an example, let's continue with Carolyn's story. Many of her friends responded well when she started focusing more on herself instead of only taking care of their needs, but some didn't. Let's look at what happened with Tammy. She had become accustomed to having Carolyn be the Caretaker with her, and she liked it. When Carolyn changed, Tammy felt hurt. She imagined that Carolyn no longer cared for her. However, she didn't say this directly; she just became snippy with Carolyn and didn't call her as often as she had.

Carolyn realized that something was wrong and decided to talk with Tammy about it. She said, "I realize that I have been overdoing my Caretaking thing with you for years, and now I am making big changes, so I can see how that would be hard for you. But I have been ignoring my own needs, and I don't want to do that anymore. I still care for you just as much as I always have; I just want to care for myself, too." Tammy listened thoughtfully and said she understood what Carolyn was trying to do. This conversation cleared things, Tammy became friendly again, and their relationship got back on a good footing.

Carolyn's friend Jane became cold and distant in reaction to Carolyn's new Self-Care behavior. When Carolyn tried to have the same kind of talk with her, Jane just got huffy and refused to listen. As a result, their friendship came to an end. Carolyn felt sadness, but she also felt OK about it. She didn't want to kill herself to maintain a friendship with someone who couldn't deal with a reciprocal relationship and couldn't talk through problems. She was content to let Jane go.

Carolyn's Relationship with Melissa

Carolyn realized that her relationship with her little sister, Melissa, was a big challenge because she was pretty sure Melissa would get angry at her if she didn't continue to caretake her. Carolyn remembered that her mother would get angry with her when she didn't take care of Melissa when they were little, so this made it even harder. However, she felt bolstered by her success with her friends and decided to take a tougher stance with Melissa anyway. Carolyn decided that she could handle Melissa's anger and wasn't going to be stopped by it.

The next evening, Melissa called in tears over an issue with her boyfriend. They'd talked about that issue many times before, and Carolyn had an early-morning meeting at her job, so she didn't want to stay up late. She told Melissa that she could only talk for fifteen minutes. She also said that it was time for Melissa to learn to take care of herself and stop looking to Carolyn to "make everything better." Melissa got angry, but Carolyn stuck to the fifteen-minute time limit. And during the conversation, she asked Melissa several times, "What do you think you should do about this issue?"

CAROLYN: "I did feel a bit guilty, but I'm clear that Melissa doesn't have a right to take so much of my time when it will cost me. And I'll tell you what, I was sure glad to get seven hours of sleep before my meeting. I felt fresh and calm, when in the past I would have talked to Melissa for hours until she calmed down, and I would only have had four hours of sleep.

"It took some time and talking with Melissa to adjust our relationship so that I could set a time limit on her without upsetting her too much. For example, I would make a suggestion earlier in our conversations about how Melissa could find other people to talk with. Eventually, we worked it out, and she doesn't rely on me overly much anymore."

As a result of Carolyn's taking better care of herself, she began to notice that she was getting more positive attention at her job and that people in general were showing her more respect.

CAROLYN: "While I liked people coming to me for help, I always admired those women who were respected by everyone. You know, the women who people wouldn't say 'boo' to, like Angelina Jolie. When I pay attention to what I need and turn away things that suck up too much energy, I feel like that kind of woman. I could get used to that!"

CHAPTER 6

The Self-Care Capacity

Self-Care is the ability to be in touch with what you want and need, and then to be able to express those wants and needs to others. With this capacity, you can speak up to get your needs met and make choices that sometimes result in your benefit.

Unlike being selfish, which would be to always put your needs and desires above anyone else's, the Self-Care Capacity helps you to see that there's health in balancing your needs with those of others. If you have a Caretaking Pattern, you may think that Self-Care is really selfishness because you have little experience with caring for your own needs and also because you may believe that it is wrong to do so. However, it only make sense that you have the right to look after your own interests as long as it doesn't prevent you from also caring about others'. In fact, you know more about your needs than anyone else could, so it makes sense that you should take care that they are met.

When you have this capacity, you can weigh what others want against what you want and make decisions about how to speak and act that are in line with your values and integrity. You find ways to make sure all your basic needs (food, sleep, self-care time, financial, and so on) are getting met. This doesn't mean you no longer care about other people, but that you value your own needs and desires at least as much as those of others.

Aspects

☐ Noticing when I feel hungry, tired, sad, scared, or need support in other ways

☐ Making choices that get my needs met

☐ Speaking up for what I want

☐ Enjoying time that is "just for me"

☐ Putting myself first sometimes

☐ Taking time to really get to know myself and how I feel

☐ Allowing myself to be supported sometimes, without feeling guilty or apologizing

☐ Understanding that I have to be sufficiently nourished, or "fueled up," before I can help anyone else

☐ Valuing myself and my needs enough that I don't let anyone take advantage of me

☐ Other aspects_____

_____

Higher Care

In the Pattern System, in addition to healthy capacities, there are higher capacities, which are the more evolved or spiritual aspects of each capacity or dimension. When you are living from a higher capacity, you embody a version of the capacity that is less egocentric and more oriented toward the good of the whole. You are living from a place that is informed by the sense that we are all connected, and you care for this larger unity.

The Higher Care Capacity is an integration of the higher aspects of Self-Care and Caring. It has the following aspects:

Caring for the Whole

You care for what is best for everyone in any given situation, including your needs and those of everyone else. This also includes the needs of the larger whole in which you are embedded, when relevant—your family, community, cultural group, and nation as well as the entire world. This also includes the needs of those with no voice—people not present who will nevertheless be affected, children, animals, and the natural world. You are concerned for their higher needs—their need for growth and development, not just what would gratify them or make them comfortable in the moment.

Which of theses aspects would you like to develop?

❒ Caring for what is best for everyone in a situation

❒ Including the needs of larger groups

❒ Including the needs of those with no voice

❒ Caring for people's higher needs

CHAPTER 7

Practicing Behavior Change

This chapter presents "real-time" practice where you can work on evoking your Self-Care Capacity to replace your Caretaking Pattern.

This is where the rubber meets the road! This is the practice that can change your Caretaking, and we have provided lots of support for you to make this happen, including the web workbook[14] and the Caretaking Online Community.[15]

Practice Outline

Here is a brief outline of the steps in this chapter:

1. Know why you want to do this practice.

2. Choose a Life Situation to practice on.

3. Know when your Caretaking gets triggered.

4. Remind yourself that Caretaking isn't necessary.

5. Create Self-Care.

6. Get support for your practice.

7. Track and improve your practice.

---

14. http://www.personalgrowthapplication.com/Pattern/Caretaking Workbook/Caretaking_Workbook.aspx
15. http://www.personal-growth-programs.com/connect

Clarifying Your Intention for Doing the Practice

Before you engage in this practice, it is helpful to clearly have in mind what you intend to gain by making this change. It is not enough to just decide that it would be a good thing to do. Figure out why you want to do it, set an intention for your practice, and keep this in mind during the week. This will help you discipline yourself to stick to the practice.

Think through the pain and difficulties caused by your Caretaking Pattern.

Notice those that will motivate you to change:

❒ I feel tired and weary from giving too much.

❒ I worry about not being able to anticipate everything people need.

❒ I set an impossible standard for myself and am tired of criticizing myself for not meeting it.

❒ I feel overwhelmed when I think of all the items for others in my to-do list and on my calendar.

❒ I feel sad that my needs aren't met.

❒ I wish other people gave me as much as I give them.

❒ I feel taken advantage of, and I'm starting to feel resentful of my loved ones.

❒ I feel guilty when other people aren't happy.

❏ Other pain and difficulties _____

_____

What do you have to gain from living from Self-Care Capacity in your life, especially those things you really want?

❏ Feeling better about myself

❏ Having my needs met (such as good rest, good health, and emotional support)

❏ Having more time to take care of myself

❏ Feeling comfortable being in balance with myself and my loved ones

❏ Feeling fulfilled and at peace

❏ Knowing I'm not responsible for how other people feel or act

❏ Other things to gain _____

_____

_____

Planning Ahead

Think of a situation that is coming up in the next week or so, or one that arises frequently, in which you want to practice the Self-Care Capacity. Or instead, think of a situation in which you typically take care of others and would like to change that. For example:

- My brother and sister-in-law want me to watch their kids for a weekend so they can have a romantic getaway.
- My friend asked me to teach her my personal bookkeeping system.
- Uncle Bob, who's a widower, asked me to help him clean and organize his garage.
- My parents want me to mediate a disagreement they're having.

Let's call this the *Life Situation*. If you aren't sure when your Caretaking Pattern gets triggered or if it seems to be around a lot of the time, just work on noticing **whenever** that pattern is activated.

As you read through the rest of this chapter, fill in your answers here or in the web workbook. The web workbook will produce a report page that tells you what you plan to do during your life to engage in this practice. You can carry this page of the web workbook with you by printing it out or keeping it on a mobile device.

You can do this practice more than once if you want to work on more than one Life Situation. You will have a different web workbook report page for each practice. If this Life Situation isn't going to come up in the next few weeks, you can do this practice by **imagining** it coming up and how you will change your behavior.

What are you afraid of in this Life Situation? For example, you might agree to watch your niece and nephew for a weekend and give up your only long stretch of downtime this month because you're afraid your brother and his wife will think you're selfish if you say no.

You may have a few specific aspects of Self-Care that you want to develop in this Life Situation. For example, you might want to develop the ability to make your personal needs a higher priority or to say no without being worried you'll be accused of being self-centered. What aspects of Self-Care do you want to develop in this Life Situation?

Set an intention to pay close attention during the Life Situation to see if your Caretaking Pattern is activated, and be prepared to practice these aspects of Self-Care instead.

What are the feelings, thoughts, or behaviors that will cue you that your Caretaking Pattern is activated? For example, I just can't say no, or I can't stand it when they're hurting, or "I know exactly what his problem is and what he should do about it," or I feel guilty that I'm not doing more, or I step in and take charge.

Remember the target fear for this Life Situation. To the extent that it isn't true, what is true instead? What are some statements that will remind you that your target fear won't really happen or that your negative perception isn't accurate? Choose from among the following statements, or create your own:

❒ My needs are just as important as everyone else's.

❒ People will still like me even if I'm not doing them favors or reading their minds.

❒ She is an adult and is capable of taking care of herself.

❒ The world will run fine without my taking care of people.

❒ I need to take care of my own health and contentment before I focus on helping anyone else.

❒ It's important for me to know how I think and feel before I act; it makes me a better person to be around.

❒ I am allowed to focus on myself, just as everyone else is.

❒ The only happiness I'm responsible for is my own.

❒ Other statements _____

_____

_____

If there is some validity to your fears or perceptions, remember the plan you devised in Chapter 5 to handle that situation. You will put that plan into action this week.

Creating Self-Care

Which of these statements will encourage you to create the aspects of Self-Care you want in this Life Situation?

❒ I deserve to receive as much as I give.

❒ I have done a great deal for others, and I know I'm good enough.

❏ I deserve to know my own wants and to give good things to myself.

❏ It's okay for me to be helped.

❏ It's good for me to devote time to myself.

❏ Other statements _____

_____

_____

You can develop an aspect of yourself that I call the Inner Champion, which supports you in being yourself and feeling good about yourself despite your fears. Your Self-Care Inner Champion encourages you to tune in to your own needs and make them your first priority.

Visit http://www.personalgrowthapplication.com/ Pattern/CaretakingWorkbook/Caretaking_Workbook_ Meditation.aspx to do a guided meditation to access your Self-Care Inner Champion.

Which of the following statements would you like your Self-Care Inner Champion to say to you?

❏ You deserve to be happy.

❏ You can have good friends who love you even if you don't caretake them.

❏ If someone loves you, they will want you to take care of yourself before helping them.

❏ Your needs and wants are very important. They matter.

❏ You can care about others without having to always help them.

❏ Your help is better when you are "filled up" yourself.

❏ People feel better about receiving when you don't over-give.

❏ You deserve to ask for and get as much support and attention from others as you have given.

❏ Other statements _____

_____

_____

What body sensation, feeling, or state of consciousness will help you evoke these aspects of Self-Care (for example, the sense of being grounded and relaxed that comes from recognizing when someone's problem is **their** issue to work out)? _____

_____

_____

_____

What image will help create Self-Care (for example, a fantastic massage or a huge bouquet of flowers)? _____

_____

_____

_____

Can any people close to you support you in creating Self-Care? What help do you want from them (for example, to remind you that your needs are as important as other people's)?

_____

_____

_____

Is there something you want people close to you to stop doing (for example, accepting your help and support without offering it in return)? _____

_____

_____

Talk to the people close to you about what they can do (or stop doing) that will help you activate the Self-Care Capacity and especially the aspects of Self-Care you want in this Life Situation.

Your Self-Care Practice Workbook Section

There is a separate section of the web workbook for helping you engage in your Self-Care Practice and keep track of it. The rest of this chapter explains how to engage in this practice and use this section.

Working with a Buddy

People have much more success with practices like this if they have a "buddy" to witness them and be their cheerleader. I recommend that you find a friend who is a good listener and who will understand what you are doing and be supportive. Or join our Caretaking Online Community,[16] where we will help you find a buddy.

After you make your plans for the practice, call your buddy and talk through what you will be doing. If you have written down specific words you want to say in the situation, practice saying them to your buddy. Even role-play the situation. For example, have your buddy play a demanding relative while you practice saying you have other plans and aren't available to help.

Set a time frame for checking in with your buddy on your progress with the practice. You could just do it once at the end of a week to report on how the practice has gone. But for even more effective support, consider checking in with your buddy every two or three days, or even every day, to let him or her know how it is going. The act of reporting in will really help to keep you on track. When you know that you'll be talking to someone about your practice, you're much more likely to do it and to keep track of what happened.

Your buddy can also support you in bringing your attention back to your own needs and feelings in situations in which you have just focused on others in the past. You can share those situations with your buddy, knowing that you will be talking to him or her about how you fared. This can be crucial support for your being accountable for your action plans and following through on them.

When the Life Situation Occurs

With some Life Situations, you know ahead of time when they will happen. For example, you know when you will

---

16. http://www.personal-growth-programs.com/connect

be attending a family celebration. In these cases, take some time right before this happens to go to Self-Care Practice Plans[17] in the web workbook (or review the pages in the paperback workbook) to review how you want to handle this Life Situation. (Keep in mind that the web workbook and the Profile Program are two different programs.) If you don't have time right before it happens, take some time earlier to prepare.

Some situations allow you to process this material **during** the Life Situation. For example, if the Life Situation involves a request from a friend, you can say you need to think about your answer, process the Caretaking impulses that are coming up, and then resume the conversation and put your plan into operation. In this case, when you take the time-out, click the above two links to review how you plan to handle the situation so you can decide what to do.

During the Life Situation, pay close attention and notice the feelings, thoughts, or behavior that will cue you that your Caretaking Pattern is activated.

If it is triggered, do the following:

- Say the statements (out loud or silently) that will remind you that you don't have to be afraid of Self-Care, or create your own on the spot.

- Put your plan into action to assert yourself around the possibility of harm or rejection.

---

17. http://www.personalgrowthapplication.com/Pattern/Care takingWorkbook/Caretaking_Workbook_Practice_Plans.aspx ?pname=LifeSituation

- Say the statements (out loud or silently) that will inspire you to create Self-Care, or create your own on the spot.

- Use a body sensation, feeling, or state of consciousness (if you have chosen one) to help create Self-Care.

- Look at the image you have chosen (if you have one) to inspire you to create Self-Care.

If you were successful in creating Self-Care, celebrate your success! Give yourself a pat on the back or a reward, such as dinner at a favorite restaurant. Appreciate yourself for this step in changing your behavior. It is very important to reinforce each step, however small, in the right direction. Your Self-Care Practice Workbook will help you in rewarding your steps toward success.

After the situation has happened, enter your Practice Notes (see below) as soon as you have time to enter what happened. Or if you don't have time, do it at the end of the day when doing your Daily Check-In Notes.

If you came up with new statements, add them to your workbook to use in the future. If you have additional insights into any of the material you have filled out previously in the workbook, feel free to add them to the pages you have already filled out.

Practice Notes

Enter your answers according to what you did in your practice. (Not all need to be answered.)

The Life Situation _____

_____

_____

The fears that came up in this situation _____

_____

_____

The aspects of Self-Care you were working on developing in this situation _____

_____

_____

What triggered the Caretaking Pattern _____

_____

_____

The statements you said to remind yourself that you don't have to be afraid of Self-Care _____

_____

_____

_____

What you did to assert yourself to handle harm or rejection _____

_____

_____

The statements you said to yourself to inspire you to create Self-Care _____

_____

_____

The body sensation, feeling, or state of consciousness you used to help create Self-Care _____

_____

_____

The image you used to inspire you to create Self-Care ____

_____

_____

How you did in attempting to create Self-Care

_____

_____

_____

Further notes on what happened _____

_____

_____

Is there anything you want to do differently next time?

_____

_____

_____

Daily Check-In

In order to remember to do this practice, it will help you to check in with yourself once a day in addition to any checking with your friend. Choose a time when you will have a few minutes to yourself and when it will be easy for you to remember to check in each day. For many people, this is right before going to bed each night or upon waking each morning. But in all cases, choose a consistent time of day that works best for you.

If the Life Situation only occurs once a week or a few times a month, you don't need to enter Daily Check-In Notes every day. Just reflect to see if it happened that day and take notes if it did. On the days it didn't happen, you don't need to do anything.

Take notes on what you were aware of that day. If the Life Situation occurred, write down what happened. Enter your notes below.

Reflect on whether the Caretaking Pattern was activated today, whether you noticed and did the practice, and what happened. _____

_____

_____

Did the Life Situation happen today? _____

_____

_____

If so, were you paying attention when it happened? _____

_____

Did the Caretaking Pattern get triggered today (in that situation or any other one)? _____

If so, did you notice when the Caretaking Pattern was triggered today? _____

If you didn't, what kept you from noticing? _____

_____

_____

What can you do tomorrow to help you be more aware?

_____

_____

_____

If you did notice that the Caretaking Pattern was triggered, did you do the practice to evoke Self-Care?

_____

If not, what stopped you from doing that? _____

_____

_____

What can you do next time to help yourself remember to evoke Self-Care? _____

_____

_____

   If you did the practice and didn't track what happened at the time, enter it under Practice Notes. If you did it more than once, take separate notes for each instance by clicking that link multiple times.

Is there anything you want to do differently tomorrow or the next time your Caretaking Pattern is triggered?

_____

_____

_____

Weekly Check-In
After a week, take notes on how this practice is working.

Day of week _____

How many times did you do the practice this week? _____

Was this enough to be helpful to you? _____

If you did the practice enough, how much of a difference did it make? _____

_____

What worked in doing the practice? _____

_____

_____

_____

What didn't work in doing the practice? _____

_____

_____

_____

Do you want to do the practice again next week? _____

Is there anything you want to do differently next week?

_____

_____

_____

CHAPTER 8

The Care Dimension

The information in this chapter will help you to get a fuller sense of the various patterns and healthy capacities that you might have with respect to care. You might learn about other patterns you want to explore and may see the relationships between your patterns and capacities. However, if you aren't interested in this level of complexity, feel free to skip this chapter or come back to it at a later time.

The Care Dimension

The Caretaking Pattern is part of the *Care Dimension* in the Pattern System. Let's look at how it is related to the other patterns and capacities.

There are three problematic patterns in the Care Dimension—Caretaking, Self-Absorbed, and Entitled.

- The **Caretaking Pattern** involves caring for and helping others to the exclusion of your own needs and even sometimes without being aware of whether they want the help.

- The **Self-Absorbed Pattern** involves being so focused on your own needs that you are unaware of other people's feelings, needs, and boundaries.

- The **Entitled Pattern** involves treating other people as extensions of yourself—as people who are only there to meet your needs.

Two healthy capacities—Caring and Self-Care—are related to these three patterns.

- **Caring** is the ability to be compassionate, nurturing, and empathic. You want the best for others and help them when needed.

- **Self-Care**, as discussed previously, is the ability to know what you need or want and be able to ask for it or take steps to get it.

Caring is a complement to Self-Care. For healthy relating, you need capacities on both sides. Caring helps you to be compassionate and giving toward others, and Self-Care helps you know and attend to your own needs and wants.

This is the nature of healthy capacities—they naturally integrate with each other, which means that they don't oppose each other. They work together; they both support your flourishing around care issues. If you have both capacities, you are able to care for and help others while at the same time taking care of yourself and asking for help when needed.

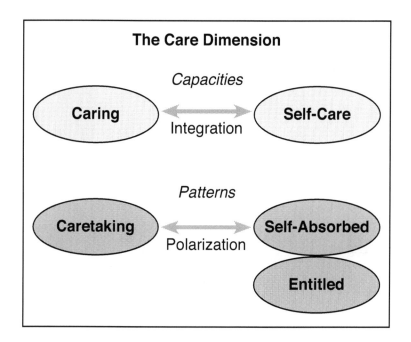

Relations Between the Patterns and Capacities

Patterns in Conflict

The patterns on the left and right sides don't integrate with each other in the way the healthy capacities do. They are polarized, which means they battle each other to determine how you relate to others. The Caretaking Pattern involves caring for and helping others to the exclusion of your own needs. However, the Self-Absorbed and Entitled Patterns involve an unhealthy or extreme focus on yourself to the exclusion of other people's feelings, needs, and boundaries. Another way to look at it is that the pattern on the left is about *under*functioning, while the patterns on the right are about *over*functioning.

Patterns Are Dysfunctional Versions of Capacities

Caring is a healthy version of Caretaking. Another way to say this is that Caretaking is an extreme, dysfunctional version of Caring. It is caring done at your own expense for ulterior motives. And the same applies on the right side. Self-Care is a healthy version of the Self-Absorbed and Entitled Patterns that involves taking care of your needs without ignoring other people's. You can say that being Self-Absorbed or Entitled is a dysfunctional version of healthy Self-Care.

Capacities Resolve Patterns

And there are even more interesting relations between the patterns and capacities. If you have a Self-Absorbed or Entitled Pattern, Caring is what you need to develop to break away from it. Thus the capacity on the opposite side of the graphic is the one needed to break from a pattern.

The same applies on the other side. If you have a Caretaking Pattern, you need Self-Care to break free from it, as we have discussed in this book.

Here is another graphic showing these relationships:

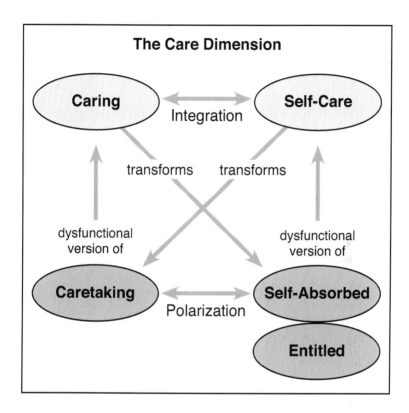

Questionnaire

It would be helpful to track which of the patterns and capacities in this dimension you have. You may have an idea from reading the descriptions, or you can take a quiz on my website. This questionnaire will give you a score for each of the patterns and capacities in the Care Dimension to help clarify how strongly you have the Caretaking Pattern or the other patterns in this dimension. It will also tell you how high you score on the healthy capacities in that dimension. To take this quiz, visit http://www.personalgrowthapplication.com/Members/Questionnaire.aspx?Questionnaire=7.

CHAPTER 9

Conclusion

Deep Healing and Transformation
of the Caretaking Pattern

When I do psychotherapy with my clients, I use Internal Family Systems Therapy (IFS), a very powerful, cutting-edge approach developed by pioneering psychologist Richard Schwartz, PhD. Since I discovered IFS a decade ago, I have seen amazing results in my clients' lives. I was developing the Pattern System for more than a decade before I discovered IFS and was thrilled to find that the two are a natural fit.

IFS work can complement the work you do on your Caretaking Pattern using this book. IFS would help you to experientially access the motivations and childhood origins behind this pattern and to heal and transform the pattern. Then your homework practice on developing your Self-Care Capacity would be even more effective. If you want to experience the most profound and lasting change in your pattern, I recommend that you practice IFS with your Caretaking Part as described below.

The IFS Model

IFS enables you to understand each of the *parts* of your psyche, sometimes called *subpersonalities*. Think of them as little people inside you. Each has its own perspective, feelings, memories, goals, and motivations. And sometimes they are at odds with each other. For example, one part of you might be trying to lose weight, and another part might want to eat whatever you want. We all have many different parts, such as the procrastinator, the lover, the inner critic, the lonely child, the rebel, the Caretaker, and so on.

If you have the Caretaking Pattern, there is a part of you that takes care of others at your own expense. You can use IFS to work on your Caretaking Part as well as any other patterns you have.

IFS recognizes that we all have child parts that are in pain, which are called *exiles*. These correspond to the wounds in the Pattern System. The parts that try to keep us from feeling this pain are called *protectors*, which correspond to the patterns.

Most important, IFS recognizes that we all have a true *Self*, which is our core healthy place or spiritual center. IFS has some innovative and easy ways to access Self. You get to know your parts and develop trusting relationships with them from the place of Self, which then leads to healing and transformation of those parts.

The IFS Process with Your Caretaking Part

IFS is an experiential therapy. You don't just get insight into your parts—you actually go inside, contact them, and have conversations with them.

What follows is a brief description of how you would do IFS with your Caretaking Part. It is just an overview to give you an idea of how the process works. The actual procedure is much more detailed and specialized. I don't expect you to be able to do IFS by reading this brief description. You will need to learn how to engage in the IFS process using my book *Self-Therapy* or courses, or by going into individual therapy with an IFS therapist (see Appendix C).

First you access your Caretaking Part experientially. You might feel it emotionally, or hear its words, or get a mental image of what it looks like. Then you access Self so that you are separate from your Caretaking Part and have a place to stand from which to connect with it. You make sure that you are open to getting to know it from its own perspective rather than judging it or wanting to get rid of it.

Then you ask it to tell you what it is trying to accomplish for you by keeping you focused on other people's needs. You want to know what it is afraid would happen if it allowed you to make your own needs a priority. This helps you to recognize the exile (wounded inner child part) that it is protecting.

This conversation will give you a good sense of how the Caretaking Part is trying to protect you, even if that protection isn't really needed anymore. This allows you to appreciate its efforts on your behalf, and your appreciation helps the Caretaking Part to trust you.

You ask the Caretaking Part for permission to work with the exile it is protecting. Then you get to know that child part and find out what happened when you were young to cause that part to be so afraid and wounded. You witness these memories in an experiential way (you may or may not know them already)—that is, you see them in a mental movie of your past. Then you enter the childhood scene and give that little child what he or she needed back then. Or you protect the wounded child part from being harmed. You might also take that part out of that harmful or painful childhood situation and into your present life, where he or she will be safe and can be connected to you and receive your love and caring.

You help the exile to release the pain and fear that he or she has been carrying all these years. Once this is done, your Caretaking Part won't feel the need to protect the exile anymore, so it can now relax and stop trying to keep you focused on other people's needs to the exclusion of your own. Then you will be able to find a healthy balance between other people's needs and your own.

My book *Self-Therapy* describes in detail how to use IFS to work through any psychological issue. See www.selfleader ship.org for detailed information about IFS and professional training in the Model. My colleagues and I also offer courses in which you can learn how to use IFS to work on yourself and do peer counseling with other people from the course. See Appendix C for IFS resources.

Conclusion

I hope this book will help you to transform your Caretaking Pattern so you can be aware of your own needs and practice the level of Self-Care that you deserve. In order for this to happen, it is important that you fully engage in the practice of creating Self-Care in Chapter 7. Reading this material and understanding yourself is an important step, but most people need to consciously work on putting this into practice in their lives.

You also may need to work on other patterns of yours in order to fully let go of Caretaking. Your Caretaking Pattern may be linked to a People-Pleasing Pattern, a Controlling Pattern, or one of the others that are mentioned in the book.

You may be able to move toward Self-Care by only focusing on your Caretaking Pattern, but you might need to do more to achieve success. If this is the case, read other books in this series, or use the web application when it becomes available, or find other ways to work on those patterns.

Don't become discouraged if your pattern doesn't transform right away. Personal growth isn't a simple, easy process, despite what some self-help books would have you believe. Letting go of a deep-seated problem takes time, effort, and a commitment to work on yourself.

Personal growth is an exciting journey, with twists and turns, painful revelations, unexpected insights, profound shifts, and an ever-deepening sense of self-awareness and mastery. I hope that this book contributes to your personal evolution and the deep satisfaction that comes from balancing caring for others with caring for yourself.

APPENDIX A

The Pattern System^{SM}

The Caretaking Pattern and the Care Dimension that contains it are just one small part of the overall Pattern System. You can use the Pattern System to obtain a complete map of your psyche. You will be able to see your strengths and your defenses, your places of pain and how you compensate for them. You'll come to understand the structure of your inner conflicts and see where you are ready to grow. The Pattern System makes clear what you need to explore next in order to resolve the issues that are most important to you.

The goal of working with the Pattern System is to live from your *True Self*, which is who you naturally are when you aren't operating from patterns and when you have developed skills for healthy relating and functioning. Self-Care is one aspect of the True Self.

A more advanced goal is to live from your *Higher Self*, which is your spiritual ground and is the integration of the higher capacities, including Higher Care.

Interpersonal Dimensions in the Pattern System

The Care Dimension is just one of ten interpersonal dimensions in the Pattern System, each containing at least two patterns and two capacities. The following are brief descriptions of some of them:

Conflict. How do you deal with differences of opinion as well as desires, disagreements, judgment, anger, and fights? Do you use avoidance tactics? Do you become angry, blaming, or defensive? Can you communicate your concerns without judgment and own your part in a problem? Do you become frightened or feel bad about yourself? Can you bring up conflicts and set limits on attacks?

Social. How do you relate to people socially? Are you outgoing or shy, scared or confident in reaching out to people or making conversation? Are you self-effacing or charming, attention seeking or avoiding? Are you overly oriented toward performance in the way you relate to others, or are you more genuine?

Care. How do you balance your needs versus other people's needs? Do you end up taking care of others rather than yourself? Do people tell you that you don't show enough care or concern for them?

Intimacy. Do you avoid intimacy, need it too much, fear it, love it? Can you be autonomous in an intimate relationship without denying your needs? Do you get overly dependent in relationships, or can you support yourself?

Power. How do you deal with power in your relationships? Do you give in too easily to others or try too hard to please them? Do you need to be in control? Do you feel as though you must stand up for yourself against people you view as dominating? Do you frustrate others without realizing why? Can you assert yourself? Can you work with people in a spirit of cooperation?

Anger and Strength. How do you deal with self-protection and assertiveness in situations that can bring up anger?

Do you dump your anger on people? Do you disown your anger and therefore lose your strength? Can you be centered and communicate clearly when you are angry? Can you be strong and forceful without being reactive?

Trust. Are you usually trusting of people, or do you easily get suspicious? Can you perceive when someone isn't trustworthy, or are you gullible?

Some additional interpersonal dimensions are:

- Honesty
- Evaluation
- Responsibility

Each of these dimensions has the same structure as the Power Dimension.

The following is a chart of all ten interpersonal dimensions and their patterns and capacities. There are two types of patterns—hard and soft. The *Hard Patterns* (on the right side) tend to be aggressive and cause other people pain, while the *Soft Patterns* (on the left side) tend to be passive and cause the person pain. If you have a Hard Pattern, you need to develop the corresponding capacity on the left side, which is a Relational Capacity. If you have a Soft Pattern, you need to develop the corresponding capacity on the right side, which is a Self-Supporting Capacity. This is, of course, just a quick summary; the interpersonal patterns will be explained in detail in a future book.

The Interpersonal Dimensions of the Pattern System℠

Jay Earley, PhD

Soft Patterns	Relational Capacities	DIMENSION	Self-Supporting Capacities	Hard Patterns
		RECEPTIVE ⟷ ACTIVE		
Dependent	Intimacy	INTIMACY	Self-Support	Distancing
Conflict-Avoiding	Good Communication	CONFLICT	Challenge, Limit Setting	Blaming, Defensive
People-Pleasing, Passive-Aggressive	Cooperation	POWER	Assertiveness	Controlling, Defiant
Caretaking	Caring	CARE	Self-Care	Self-Absorbed, Entitled
Self-Effacing	Genuineness	SOCIAL	Social Confidence	Charmer
Disowned Anger	Centeredness	STRENGTH	Strength	Angry
Gullible	Trust	TRUST	Perceptiveness	Suspicious
Deceptive	Tact	HONESTY	Honesty	Judgmental
Idealizing	Appreciation	EVALUATION	Perceptiveness	Judgmental
Victim, Powerless	Vulnerability	RESPONSIBILITY	Responsibility	Controlling

There will be a book on each of the interpersonal patterns. Visit http://www.personal-growth-programs.com/pattern-system/pattern-system-series to see which ones are available now.

Personal Dimensions in the Pattern System

The Pattern System also deals with a variety of personal patterns. The following are brief descriptions of some of them:

Self-Esteem. Do you feel good about yourself, or do you constantly judge yourself? Do you accept yourself as you are? Do you try to prop up your self-esteem with pride? How do you deal with improving yourself?

Accomplishment. Are you confident in working on and accomplishing tasks? Do you procrastinate? Do you push or judge yourself to try to get things done or to achieve, or can you accomplish with ease?

Pleasure. How do you deal with food, drink, sex, and other bodily pleasures? Do you indulge in harmful ways? Do you control yourself rigidly to avoid doing that? Do you bounce back and forth between overindulging and castigating yourself for that?

Some further personal dimensions are:

- Action
- Change
- Hope
- Excellence
- Decision
- Risk
- Rationality/Emotion

Each of these dimensions has the same structure as the Care Dimension. There will be a book on each of the patterns in each dimension. Visit http://www.personal-growth-pro grams.com/pattern-system/pattern-system-series to see which ones are available now.

Wounds

The following are the main wounds:

Deficit Wounds

1. Deprivation Wound
2. Abandonment Wound
3. Rejection Wound
4. Not Seen Wound

Harm Wounds

1. Judgment Wound
2. Shame Wound
3. Domination Wound
4. Guilt Wound
5. Violation Wound
6. Attack Wound
7. Betrayal Wound
8. Exploitation Wound

Deficiency Wounds

1. Unlovable Wound
2. Inadequate Wound
3. Depressed Wound
4. Basic Deficiency Wound

Motivations

The following are some of the important motivations:

- Fear of Harm
- Fear of Rejection
- Fear of Losing Yourself
- Attempt to Stop Harm
- Attempt to Stop Pain
- Attempt to Get Connection
- Fear of Success
- Fear of Failure
- Opposition to a Parent

An Open-Ended System

The Pattern System is open-ended. We sometimes add new patterns, subpatterns, capacities, and dimensions, or even new types of patterns. We welcome input from other people in developing the Pattern System further. See http://thepatternsystem.wikispaces.com for a fuller outline of the system.

Definitions of Terms

Dimension. An area of psychological functioning (e.g., power, intimacy, or self-esteem) that contains certain patterns and capacities that deal with similar issues.

Healthy Capacity. A way of behaving or feeling that makes your life productive, connected, and happy. An aspect of the True Self.

Higher Self. Your spiritual ground and the integration of your higher capacities.

Inner Champion. An aspect of yourself that supports and encourages you and helps you feel good about yourself. It is the magic bullet for dealing with the negative impact of the Inner Critic.

Inner Critic. A part of you that judges you, demeans you, and pushes you to do things. It tends to make you feel bad about yourself.

Interpersonal Pattern. A pattern that involves interpersonal relating.

Life Situation. A situation that is coming up in the next week or two in which you will have the opportunity to practice creating a healthy capacity instead of prolonging a pattern.

Motivation. A kind of underlying intention (e.g., fear of harm or desire for approval) that drives a pattern.

Pattern. A way of behaving or feeling that is a problem for you or others (e.g., being dependent, controlling, or judgmental). A pattern tends to be too rigid, extreme, dysfunctional, or inappropriate for the situation you are in.

Polarization. A dynamic in which two patterns are fighting each other to determine how you behave or relate to others.

True Self. Who you naturally are when you aren't operating from patterns and when you have developed skills for healthy relating and functioning. The healthy capacities are aspects of the True Self.

Wound. A harmful or traumatic way you were treated, usually in childhood (e.g., being neglected, hit, or dismissed).

Resources

Books

Self-Therapy, by Jay Earley. How to do Internal Family Systems (IFS) sessions on your own or with a partner. Also a manual of the IFS method that can be used by therapists.

Self-Therapy for Your Inner Critic, by Jay Earley and Bonnie Weiss. Applies IFS to working with Inner Critic parts.

Resolving Inner Conflict, by Jay Earley. How to work with polarization using IFS.

Working with Anger in IFS, by Jay Earley. How to work with too much anger or disowned anger using IFS.

Activating Your Inner Champion Instead of Your Inner Critic, by Jay Earley and Bonnie Weiss. How to bring forth your Inner Champion to deal with attacks from your Inner Critic.

Embracing Intimacy, by Jay Earley. How to work through blocks that keep you from having the intimacy you want in your love relationship.

Letting Go of Perfectionism, by Jay Earley and Bonnie Weiss. How to work through fears that lead to perfectionism so you can have more ease and perspective in your life.

Taking Action, by Jay Earley. How to work through procrastination and achieve your goals.

A Pleaser No Longer, by Jay Earley. How to work through your tendency to please people and learn to be assertive instead.

A series of Pattern System books similar to this one will be published over the next few years. A list of the currently available Pattern System books will be maintained and updated at http://www.personal-growth-programs.com/pattern-system-series.

Updates for this book. Visit http://www.personal-growth-programs.com/beyond-caretaking-owners to register yourself as an owner of this book. You will receive an updated version of the ebook whenever it is improved. You will also be notified about each new book in the series as it comes out.

Courses

My colleagues and I teach telephone courses on perfectionism, procrastination, and many of the other topics of the Pattern System books. We also teach telephone courses on IFS for the general public. My website http://www.personal-growth-programs.com has the details.

Websites and Applications

My IFS website (with Bonnie Weiss), http://www.personal-growth-programs.com, contains popular and professional articles on IFS and its application to various psychological issues. You can also sign up for our email list to receive future articles and notifications of upcoming courses and groups.

My personal website, http://www.jayearley.com, contains more of my writings and information about my psychotherapy practice, including my therapy groups.

Our other website, http://www.psychemaps.com, contains a questionnaire to determine which of the seven types of Inner Critics you have and a program to profile your Inner Critic and Inner Champion.

The Caretaking Online Community (http://www.personal-growth-programs.com/connect) is for people who are reading this book and would like to support each other in letting go of Caretaking. It is part of a larger online community of people who are working on various aspects of their personal growth and healing through our books, websites, and programs.

The Pattern System website, http://thepatternsystem.wikispaces.com, contains an outline of the latest version.

I am also developing a web application based on the Pattern System and IFS that will allow people to explore their psychological issues and do self-therapy.

The Center for Self-Leadership is the official IFS organization. Its website, http://www.selfleadership.org, contains IFS articles, trainings, workshops, and a list of IFS therapists.

Books and Booklets by
Jay Earley, PhD

The IFS Series
Self-Therapy
Self-Therapy for Your Inner Critic (with Bonnie Weiss)
Resolving Inner Conflict
Working with Anger in IFS
Negotiating for Self-Leadership

The Pattern System Series
Embracing Intimacy
Letting Go of Perfectionism (with Bonnie Weiss)
Taking Action: Working Through Procrastination
and Achieving Your Goals
A Pleaser No Longer
Beyond Caretaking

The Inner Critic Series (with Bonnie Weiss)
Self-Therapy for Your Inner Critic
Activating Your Inner Champion
in Place of Your Inner Critic
Letting Go of Perfectionism

Other Books
Interactive Group Therapy
Transforming Human Culture
Inner Journeys

11550091R00062

Printed in Great Britain
by Amazon.co.uk, Ltd.,
Marston Gate.